BABY ANIMALS

An Animal Information Book

PRICE/STERN/SLOAN
Publishers, Inc., Los Angeles
1984

Baby deer are called fawns.

For the first few months, fawns have white spots on their reddish coats. This helps them blend into the woods so that they are difficult for other animals to find.

Foals are baby horses.

Only a few hours after they are born, they stand up and walk around.

Foals are playful and love to run. Sometimes they will run far from their mothers, but they always come back.

Donkey babies are called foals, too.

Donkeys and horses are members of the same family. Donkey foals are very much like horse foals.

When they live in the wild, they stay with their mothers for about a year.

A monkey baby holds on to its mother when she moves. When the baby is very young, it holds on to the fur on her stomach. As the baby grows older and stronger, it rides on its mother's back.

Coyote babies are called pups.

A coyote mother has many pups at once.

They live together in a den that is either a hole in the ground or a hidden place among rocks.

Baby cats are called kittens.

Kittens are very playful animals.
They like to play with other
kittens, and they love to play
with anything that moves.

Kittens grow up very quickly.

Elephant babies are called calves.

Like adult elephants, elephant calves are very large. Calves may weigh up to 300 pounds when they are born.

They stay with their mothers for several years until they are ready to be on their own.

Baby leopards are called cubs.

Leopards are members of the cat family.

Even young cubs are very good at climbing trees.

Leopard cubs stay with their mothers a long time.

Although they are small now, these peregrine falcon chicks will grow up to be about 17 inches long.

They are beginning to lose the white feathers they were born with and to grow the darker feathers adult falcons have.

Baby sheep are called lambs.

Sheep usually have only one lamb at a time.

Lambs are born early in the spring.

Lambs stay with their mothers until they are about six months old.

Jaguars are members of the cat family.

Jaguar mothers take care of their cubs the way cats take care of kittens.

When the mother wants to move her cubs, she uses her mouth to pick them up at the back of their necks.

Baby pigs are called piglets.

A mother pig is called a sow.

She has many piglets at a time.

Piglets born at the same time are called litters.

Until they are several weeks old, piglets stay very close to their mothers.

Baby swans are called cygnets. They are born with brown and gray feathers. As they grow older, they lose these feathers and grow white feathers.

Baby cows are called calves.

When they are only a few hours old, calves will stand up and try to walk around.

Calves stay with their mothers until they are between six and eight months old.

Llama mothers take good care of their babies. They provide food for them, and they protect them.

This llama baby is almost old enough to leave its mother.

Animal Information Books
Titles in this Series

Copyright © 1984 Ottenheimer Publishers, Inc.
Published by Price/Stern/Sloan Publishers, Inc.,
410 North La Cienega Boulevard, Los Angeles, California 90048
All Rights Reserved.
Printed in Brazil.
ISBN: 0-8431-1512-2